Justin Burakali Bayongwa

Hospital information systems

Justin Burakali Bayongwa

Hospital information systems

Analysis of the hospital information system in the DRC: the case of New Hope Hospital

Imprint

Any brand names and product names mentioned in this book are subject to trademark, brand or patent protection and are trademarks or registered trademarks of their respective holders. The use of brand names, product names, common names, trade names, product descriptions etc. even without a particular marking in this work is in no way to be construed to mean that such names may be regarded as unrestricted in respect of trademark and brand protection legislation and could thus be used by anyone.

Cover image: www.ingimage.com

This book is a translation from the original published under ISBN 978-620-2-55111-3.

Publisher:
Sciencia Scripts
is a trademark of
International Book Market Service Ltd., member of OmniScriptum Publishing Group
17 Meldrum Street, Beau Bassin 71504, Mauritius
Printed at: see last page
ISBN: 978-620-3-31813-5

Analysis of the hospital information system in the DRC: Case of New Hope Hospital

Dedication

- To our dear family BAYONGWA LUGALIKA ;
- At the Free University of the Great Lakes (ULGL) in Bukavu.

Acknowledgements

Our thanks go first and foremost to the Eternal God, our Almighty Father, Creator and Supreme Chief, Master of times and circumstances. May power, honour and glory be his!

We also thank our parents and brothers and sisters, their contribution is enormous.

The Free University of the Great Lakes in general, and the Faculty of Economics and Management Informatics played the primary role in our comprehensive training. It is from this great private accredited university that we have acquired the solid scientific background that allows us to carry out scientific research on a daily basis. We have inherited from her a sound knowledge of Business Informatics, in witness of which we pay her vibrant tributes through this paragraph; to Professor MUGISHO KATENGURA Christian. Find here the expression of our feelings of deep gratitude!

To all the administrative and nursing staff of New Hope Hospital, and to everyone who has contributed to the collection of the data needed for this work, we are grateful!

What do friends, colleagues and acquaintances and the Editions Universitaires Europeennes (the publishing house of this book) find in the present letter the expression of our feelings of gratitude!

Acronyms and abbreviations

AEDES: Agency Еигорёеппе for the Пёye1oppeшeп1 and the 8ап1ё ;
BDD : Data base ;
CHU : University Hospital Centre ;
CODEPO: Cooperation Unit of the Ecole polytechnique ;
CS: Centre of santë ;
DGOS: General Directorate of Healthcare Provision ;
Dr.: Doctor ;
HRM: Human Resources Management.
HGR: Hospital Gënëra1 from Rëfërence ;
HPGR: Hopital Provincial Gënëra1 from Rëfërence ;
GI: Management Information Systems ;
L1 : Premi dre липёe de Licence ;
L2 : Second aniK'e of Licence ;
NHH: New Hope Hospital ;
NICT: New Information and Communication Technologies ;
ENT: Otorhinolaryngology ;
DRC: Rëpub1ique Dëmocratique from Congo ;
HR: Human Resources ;
DBMS : Database management system;
SI: Information system ;
HIS: Hospital Information System ;
SQL : Structured Query Language ;
TP : Practical work ;
ULB : Free Universe of Brussels ;
ULGL : Free Universe of Great Lakes ;
ZS : Zone of santë ;

Resume

The health sector is a very important part of the public service. If the health of the population remains the priority of the State. A computer scientist researcher is interested in the quality of hospital information systems, because they contribute to the performance of the health structure.

Indeed, studies have shown that the majority of hospitals in the Democratic Republic of Congo use the traditional method (paper and pencil) to register patients, and drawers to archive and file files, so our research targeted New Hope Hospital, a large private hospital in the province of South Kivu.

Analysis of the hospital information system at New Hope Hospital reveals that its HIS is manual. This analysis was done using both the analytical and the structural-functional methods. These two methods enriched by techniques: observation, documentation, interview, etc. have made the web one of the main sources of information.

In order to overcome this problem, we have proposed medical software packages (software) that already exist elsewhere and that are applicable in the health sector: CERHIS, OpenClinic GA, Patient OS, etc. And we have recommended computerisation projects that are essential to the HIS of the Dtudid medical centre in particular, and of the DRC in general, so that HIS can contribute to the performance of the country's health structures, obviously through computerisation.

v

Abstract

The Health sector is a very important one to the public function. If the health of people stays the priority of the State, a computer scientist is interested in the quality of hospital information systems, because these contribute to the performance of a health organization.

In fact, anterior studies have proven that most of hospitals in Democratic Republic of Congo use traditional methods (sheets of paper and pens) to register patients, and to the shelves to archive and rank records. Our research has taken as sample New Hope Hospital, a great private hospital in SUD-KIVU.

The Analysis made about the hospital information system of New Hope Hospital bring to light that its information system is handmade. The study has been conducted with the analytical and stucture-functional methods, powered by the techniques : contemplation, documentation, interview, ... and the web as main source of information.

To solve the discovered weakness, we have suggested medical applications commonly used elsewhere in the sector of health. Among these softwares, we have cited : CERHIS, OpenClinic GA, Patient Os, and the like. In the end, we have also recomended indispensable projects of digitalization for New Hope Hospital in particular, and DRC in general, so that from then on the hospital information systems contibute to the performance of the country health organizations, of course through the digitalization.

Justin BURAKALI Bayongwa

General introduction

1. Context and issues

In дёр11 a health structure is a company because of its special nature. It must be governed by the enterprise system, as set out in mëthode MERISE.

The company brings together a set of material, immatëriels, financial and human resources gathered to produce and sell goods and services on a marclm to make a profit (Nalliat, s.d.).

In this context, there are three sub-systems in a health structure, as in any company:

- The *steering system,* consilium of the members of the board of directors, which dëfinissent the general policy of the company, the objectives to be achieved, the organisational strategy, the necessary resources, and controls their execution;
- The *operating system* consists of essentially human resources that exëeutent or that carry out the tasks dëfinies by the management through the resources matërielles and immatërielles placed at their disposal;
- The *information system,* which is a "set organisë of resources: matëriel, software, personnel, data, procëdures ; allowing to acquire, process, store, communicate information (data, texts, images, sounds...) in organisations" (Reix, 1995).

In the light of the above, whatever their disciplines, the authors agree that the information system is *the backbone,* the *hinge of* any company, all the more so as it constitutes the junction, the bridge and the communication channel between the steering system and the system for better management of the company.

The probtematic of information systems is essentially based on the granularity of the information that needs to be managed within the company: (e.g. personnel, matëriels, relations intërieures and extërieures, accounts, finances, and other data); however, the complexity of the development of probtematics is also a particularly complex feature of HIS for reasons such as the many spëcificitës in the santë sector, the complexity and development of organisations, the diversity and complexity of business processes and the importance of national specificities (Sabrina, 2015).

In technologically developed countries, HIS are computerised, whereas in Rëpublique Dëmocratique from Congo to gënëral, and in particular the city of Bukavu, the health structures are still lagging behind in terms of amëlioration in the quality of their information systems.

In France, for example, in order to make IS more efficient, particularly in terms of quality and safety of care, the General Directorate for the Provision of Care (DGOS) launched the *digital hospital* programme in November 2011 (Ministere des Solidarires et de la Santë, 2011). The stratëgie hospital numërique in France, dëfinit a plan for dëveloppement and the modernisation of hospital information systems and aims to set priorities and objectives for 6 years, mobilising all the players concerned and supporting the ëtablissements de santd in their transformation through information and communication technologies (2011).

New Hope Hospital, which is a modern health structure with two networks of hospitals in different areas, has not made enough progress in the automation of its information system. Our experience at New Hope Hospital and the investigations carried out on its HIS, reveal that it suffers from the following:

- The use of pen and paper for the transcription of the information per service;

- Lack of a database for the optimal management of hospital data;
- Lack of applications and websites for specific purposes;
- No intranet or other types of local networks to interconnect services and agencies;
    - Lack of technology for digital patient monitoring and follow-up;
    - Absence of an IT department and IT master plan ;
    - Manual management of patient files ;
    - Mostly manual invoicing ;
    - Hand-held records and consumption sheets;
- Manual management of personnel files and counters of private and public partners, etc.

The above weaknesses raise the following questions:

- ❖ *What information system exists within New Hope Hospital?*
- ❖ *What can be the optimal information system to provide the latter with for the rational management of its data and the increased monitoring of patients?*

2. *Assumptions:*

- ❖ Despite the presence of computers, printers, scanners, office software and other electronic equipment available at New Hope Hospital, given the absence of appropriate applications and databases for automatic data processing, *the existing information system at New Hope Hospital would be manual.*
- ❖ Given the granularity of the information to be managed in this hospital, the total treatment by man exposes him to risks that are no longer to be demonstrated, *a computerised information system would be the most appropriate for rational data management and increased patient monitoring.*

3. *Status of the issue*

The hospital information system is of interest to several disciplines and there are several researchers on the subject.

Conscious of the above, we have explored the existing literature, and the following works have caught our attention:

1) S. Guetibi, *Developpement du système d'information hospitalier par l'un des huit principes du management qualite* (doctoral research project), March 2015, Sidi Mohamed Ben University.

Sabrina's research project focuses on two areas: quality management in health care institutions, and hospital information systems. Quality management has become essential in the management of a health care institution in order to cope with structural, social, ethical and financial constraints. This quality of care, the very essence of the values of quality management, according to WHO cited by Sabrina; the policy is to make all the players understand that the objective is to ensure the best service at the best cost for the benefit of the greatest number of people (p. 6). As for the HIS, it now constitutes a major lever for encouraging the coordination of professionals in the hospital sector both within and outside establishments, for improving the quality and safety of care, and for optimising the use of the resources of health establishments (Idem).

The main objective of this work is to use the process approach to make the HIS evolve according to the evolution of the hospital, studying the case of the University Hospital of Fes, and introducing this approach in all the stages of the development of this system, in order to reach the final objective of "Good" change or continuous improvement (Idem).

What this work has in common with our own is the quality of information systems in hospitals and the approach used to diagnose risks and propose solutions. Nevertheless, there is a significant difference between the present work and Sabrina's, in that her orientations focus on the postulates of Public Health in terms of information systems, whereas in our context we want to involve information technology in the hospital environment to improve the quality of HIS.

2) Cheik O. Bagayoko, *Mise en place d'un Systeme d'Information Hospitalier en Afrique Francophone: Cinz@n, study and validation of the model in Mali* (These de doctorat, Universite de la Mediterranee), 04/10/2010.

Within the framework of this project, Oumar proposes to lay the foundations of a simple, adapted, economically and culturally acceptable model of a computerised hospital information system, with reference to the model implemented at the Hopital Mere Enfant le "Luxembourg" in Mali, in collaboration with the hospital authorities and all potential actors. Its approach is based on the valorisation of Open Source tools (Oumar, 2010).

Indeed, we have a common objective with Cheick: we advocate the implementation of computerised information systems in hospital centres. In this context, NICTs constitute a vector favouring the coordination of health professionals, the optimisation of health expenditure through better coordination of care processes, and close cooperation to enable better patient care (p. 1).

On the other hand, our contribution is to direct our ideas towards hospital data management, patient records, security, and patient monitoring, in order to encourage the automation of HIS in the Democratic Republic of Congo in general, and at New Hope Hospital in particular.

3) J. Burakali B.: *Proposal for the design and implementation of a digital home security system in a city: case of the alert of attacks and home intrusions by*

4) *n the city of Bukavu* (Travail de Memoire), Free University of the Great Lakes (ULGL) of Bukavu, November 2020.

We have used this previous research because it proposes a computerised information system for home security by means of facial recognition and real-time alerts, but it is worth recalling that in the context of increased surveillance of patients in a hospital, of the movements of individuals within it, healthcare professionals also need a digital security system. However, the peculiarity of the present work is that it moves away from the security logic of residential homes to focus on security in a medical structure, and specifically NEW HOPE HOSPITAL.

5) Mr. Abdoul Aziza BA, Implementation of *a web application for the management of patients of the Internal Medicine Department at the Regional Hospital Center EL HADJI AHMADOU SAKHIR NDIEGUENE DE THIES* (Memory), Alioune Diop University of Bambey - Professional License 2020

In his work, the author analyses the information system existing in the hospital's **Internal Medicine** Department, and diagnoses the following limitations:

- A waste of time in the patient's consultation ;
- Recurrent redundancy in the input of information.

Hence, he proposes as a solution, an automated information system that will improve the patient management system and further motivate the staff thanks to interfaces designed in a logical and functional manner that is easy to understand (M. Abdoul, 2020).

The result achieved by Mr. Abdoul will interest our work by the fact that the web application that he proposed to the studied structure will be an element of the solutions in the scope of our research essentially focused on New Hope Hospital.

6) Samar Bakoben, *Patient management in a clinic in Java* (Memory) ? Lebanese University-Lebanese Degree in Management Informatics, 2009.

Having diagnosed the use of traditional methods (paper and pencils) in the management of patient files, it seemed essential to Samar to find an indispensable solution, which is used to :

- Organising the Doctor's Schedule ;
- Manage patient appointments and reservations;
- To computerise patient files, recording all the details of their visits (examinations, results, prescriptions) on the computer;
- Print medical reports instead of writing them by hand;
- Search for records in a second (Bakoben, 2009).

Samar's memoir work seems very interesting to us in that it is more focused on the computerized management of patient records, and it is on this point that we are concentrating a lot of our work to encourage the computerization of patient records management in health structures in the Democratic Republic of Congo in general, and within New Hope Hospital in particular.

7) Universite Libre de Bruxelles, *Cerhis, IT tools adapted for the management of hospitals in the DRC* (article consulted on https://www.ulb-cooperation.org/fr/actualites on 03/02/2021 at 10:00 am Bukavu time).

This article produced and published by ULB describes the CERHIS software, which is one of the rare IT tools for managing hospital patient files, and which takes into account the many technical constraints encountered in hospitals in developing countries (ULB-Cooperation, 2019).

In a large majority of hospitals in the DRC, according to the article, patient files are kept on paper, which poses enormous problems of filing and storage. Access to old information is difficult, if not impossible. Important and sometimes vital information is regularly lost, not only to the detriment of the quality of patient care, but also to the general management of the structure (p. 1).

This is the motivation, according to the source, for the conception and realisation of Cerhis as a computer tool to help manage patient files in hospitals in the DRC. This work is dear to us insofar as it constitutes an element of the set of solutions envisaged in the conduct of this project to obtain computerised HIS in the health structures of the DRC in general, and of New Hope Hospital in particular.

8) S. Nacera; T. Siham, *Hospital Information System and Hospital Performance: Close links. Case of CHUde Mohamed-Lamine Debaghine* (Memoire), Master 2018

With the objective of demonstrating that there is an impact of HIS on the managerial performance of the Bab El Oued University Hospital, through a qualitative study at the level of the ad hoc structure by means of non-directive interviews, Nacera and Siham concluded a :

- The use of IS in the collection and dissemination of information necessary to make decisions appropriate to the different problems of managing different services;

- The existence of the impact of HIS on the hospital centre's managerial performance.

In this context, we will use the results of this Master's thesis, with scientific evidence to support our arguments that the information system remains the backbone of any structure, and specifically the health structure.

As for us, our work focuses on the *Analysis of the Hospital Information System in the DRC: the case of NEW HOPE HOSPITAL,* where we analyse the quality of the hospital information system of the medical centre under study and compare it to normal situations elsewhere, in order to propose progressive and sustainable solutions for better medical care in the Democratic Republic of Congo in general, and within New Hope Hospital in particular.

4. *Aims of the work*

a) Overall objective :

Overall, the objective of this work is to assess the existing information system within New Hope Hospital, diagnose the risks and propose progressive and sustainable solutions for the improvement of the quality of HIS, not only for New Hope Hospital, but also for all health structures in the Democratic Republic of Congo.

b) Specific objectives

Specifically, the idea is to propose the implementation of a computerised HIS that will make it possible to:

- To computerise patient files, recording all the details of their visits (examinations, results, prescriptions) on the computer;
    - Print medical reports instead of writing them by hand;
    - Search for files in a second ;
- Easy access to the files of newly admitted patients (history, antecedents, diagnosis, treatments, etc.);
- Keep important data in scientifically very well congested databases;
    - Interconnect the different hospital structures;
    - Interconnecting the different" services ;
    - Computerised monitoring of hospital patients;
    - Ensuring the safety of patients and nursing staff;
- Automatically follow the patient's progress and stay in contact with him/her after admission;
- Print consumption statements and invoices automatically generated by the related applications.

5. *Choice and interest of the subject*

"The IS is becoming a vector for change in the skills of the organisation's agents and its design assumes that it will have an impact of the information system on the performance of the organisation's services" (Saidani & Taleb, 2018).

As human health is at the forefront, health professionals who save human lives need to be aware of the impact of HIS on the performance of their services. In this context, as computer scientists that we are, we are motivated by research in the field of health within the framework of hospital informatics in order to contribute to the best medical care in the heads of health professionals.

From a personal point of view, we have an interest in establishing IT in hospitals, hence our contribution as citizens to the public service in charge of public health.

From a social point of view, the appropriation of the results of this work will enable health professionals to ensure better care for patients, and thus reduce the mortality rate of the population, because when there is poor care, there is a high mortality rate of the population due to a lack of appropriate care; this also becomes beneficial for the Government of the DRC.

From a pedagogical and scientific point of view, this work will greatly motivate computer science students, especially those in the field of Information System Design, to realise that they are really omnipotent in the community. Moreover, this work will add to the stock of computer knowledge, and more particularly hospital computer science.

6. *Spatial and temporal delimitation*

Spatially, this work focuses on the health sector in the Democratic Republic of Congo, and more specifically on the NEW HOPE HOSPITAL medical centre.

In terms of time, the study focuses on the years 2019-2021, because already in 2019 we had a very solid and coherent scientific background in the field of information systems, and since 2020 we are moving into the health sector (New Hope Hospital agent).

From an analytical point of view, only the information system will be retained in our study.

7. *Methodology*

In order to successfully achieve our results, we mainly used the analytical and structural-functional methods that allowed us to analyse and understand the business processes within the framework of the existing IS at New Hope Hospital.

Techniques such as observation, interviews, documentation and webography played an important role during the explorations.

8. *Division of labour*

In addition to the introduction and the conclusion, this book is developed in 4 chapters, namely:

- The first chapter deals with the *theoretical framework:* Generalities about information systems in hospitals and the contribution of HIS to improving hospital performance.
- The second chapter deals with the *presentation of the study environment: A* brief description of New Hope Hospital.
- *The* third chapter is devoted to the *study of the existing information system* within New Hope Hospital.
- The fourth chapter deals with the *proposal of solutions*: Existing solutions (clinical software) and project solutions.

Chapter 1: THEORICAL FRAMEWORK

1.0 Introduction

From the Master's thesis of SAIDANI Nacera and TALEB Siham, *Hospital Information System and Hospital Performance: close links. Case of Mohamed Lamine Debaghine's CHU*, this chapter develops two sections to know:
- The information system in public hospitals;
- The contribution of the HIS to improving hospital performance.

1.1. *The information system in public hospitals.*

Public health establishments are encouraged to question their practices by modifying their organisation in order to guarantee the quality of patient services while controlling costs and optimising the use of resources. However, the evolution of professional practice and organisation has not kept pace, and a gap has emerged between regulation and professional practice. These institutions have to adapt to new management rules in order to minimise costs.

Among the management tools in health care institutions: the Information System (IS), which is increasingly evolving, this is linked to the complexity and development of organisations.

There are IS evolution projects, which reconfigure information and decision-making circuits, and which are designed as levers for optimising the performance of public or private organisations. According to Bonnet & Vauquier, "The IS to be rebuilt will be of a new kind. It must be capable of adapting to multiple organisational, business and technical changes over long periods of time, several decades. This IS will be able to recycle itself more naturally than our old systems, it will be more agile and will allow a better alignment of the business with the software. It will be a more sustainable IS".

This information system is defined by Laudon, K and Laudon, J as follows: "an information system is a set of interrelated components that collect, process, store and disseminate information to assist decision-making, coordination and control within the organization" (Kenneth; Fimbel; Eric quoted by Saidani & Taleb).

Section 1: General information on hospital information systems.

In the field of medicine and health in general, computerisation has been implemented in all health care institutions for almost thirty years and is an integral part of health policy. Information is considered to be the raw material, and in order to make rational use of it, it has become necessary to have a real information system that allows the provision of necessary and relevant information in real time. The presentation of the HIS concept requires a return to the general definition of the information system in order to approach this concept in the context of health establishments.

1.1. Information and the information system

In the fields of information technology and telecommunications, the IS concept now applies to all organisations, private or public.

The importance of information systems in companies and administrations is to demonstrate how to set up and manage a quality, efficient information system at the best cost while taking on the business constraints.

An Information System represents all the elements involved in the management, processing, transport and dissemination of information within the organisation. Very concretely, the scope of the term Information System can be very different from one organisation to another.

1.1.1 The system

According to the founding father of the general theory of systems, Von Bertalanffy, the system is "a set of reciprocal exchanges with an environment, these exchanges ensuring a certain autonomy. A set of interacting sub-systems, this interdependence ensuring a certain coherence. A set undergoing more or less profound modifications over time while maintaining a certain permanence".

According to Joel de ROSNAY, the system is "a set of dynamically interacting elements organised according to a goal".

According to Edgar Morin, a system constitutes "a global unit, organised of interrelationships between elements, actions and individuals".

1.1.2 The information

Information is a basic element for steering an organisation, so it is necessary to collect, process and disseminate this information. Indeed, information is the key element of an information system, in addition to the definition given by Laudon, K and Laudon, J, information is "a set of data, which is received by a human being who interprets it. It is also an element of knowledge that can be coded for storage, processing or communication".

Information differs from data in that it fulfils a role. Data is raw and has no dimension, whereas information has a specific meaning.

Data becomes information when it is contextualised. On the other hand, knowledge, for Nonaka, Toyama and Kanno, "is a dynamic process created through social interaction between the individual and the organisation. Knowledge is context specific".

According to Darbelet (Michel), Izard (Laurent) and Scaramuzza (Michel): "Information represents data transformed into a meaningful form for the person who receives it, it has a real value for his decisions and actions".

According to Nasr (Philip) defines information as: "a picture of objects and facts, it represents them and corrects or confirms the idea we had of them. It transforms an item of information, a data into a resource that can be used by the addressee".

The difficulty in defining this concept lies in its use by several fields, adding to its confusion with other concepts (data, knowledge) which seem to be synonyms, which is not true. In order to clarify these concepts and eliminate this confusion, we will define the three concepts:

• Data: "A data is a representation of information in a program: either in the text of the program (source code) or in memory during execution. Data, often coded, describes the elements of software such as an entity (thing), an interaction, a transaction, an event, a subsystem (Wikipedia). In short, data are characters or symbols on which computers can perform operations. Data is therefore an element of information, or information in itself, that can be processed by a computer.

• Information: "Information is the collection of useful data, capable of providing knowledge or information about a particular way. Information comes from data, and therefore data are not based on information" (difference- between-data-and-information, 2018). In short, **Information=Data + Meaning.**

Data processing (setting)

Figure 1: Illustrative figure showing the difference between data and information

• Knowledge: is the set of notions and principles that a person acquires through study, observation or experience. Knowledge comes from the minds at work.

As a result, within the hospital, according to the actors, the conception of information is variously lost in this way: For the nursing staff, information is the essence of their job, because the information gathered on patients will enable them to better orientate their diagnosis and therapy. For managers, the information collected on patients is the tool for steering the institution's policy.

1.1.3 Definition of the SI

An IS is a construction consisting of information, processing, organisational rules and human and technical resources. The sets of information are partial representations of facts that are of interest to the institution, organisation or company.

The definition of the information system varies according to the authors.

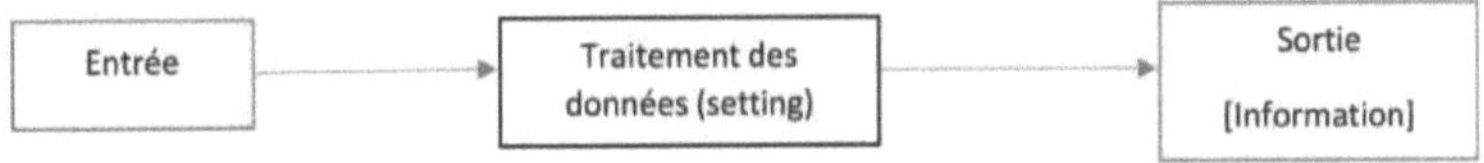

According to Laudon K and Laudon J, the information system is "a set of interrelated components that collect information, process, store and disseminate it to assist in decision-making, coordination and control within the organisation".

According to Robert Reix, the information system is an "organised set of resources: hardware, software, personnel, data, procedures... enabling information (in the form of data, text, images, sounds, etc.) to be acquired, processed and stored within and between organisations".

It is essential, therefore, to stress that the concept of IS is not just computer science, whereas in general terms we tend to identify information systems and computer science.

The widespread majority opinion is that an organisation's information system can be summed up as a set of IT tools. However, although this is the majority opinion, it is in fact wrong. There is indeed a close relationship between IS and IT. However, it is not a relationship of identity but one of demand and supply. Indeed, there is a need in organisations to process information to enable them to be efficient and to develop. It so happens that information technology can offer tools to satisfy these needs in an adapted way. The relationship between the IS and IT is therefore of the client-supplier type.

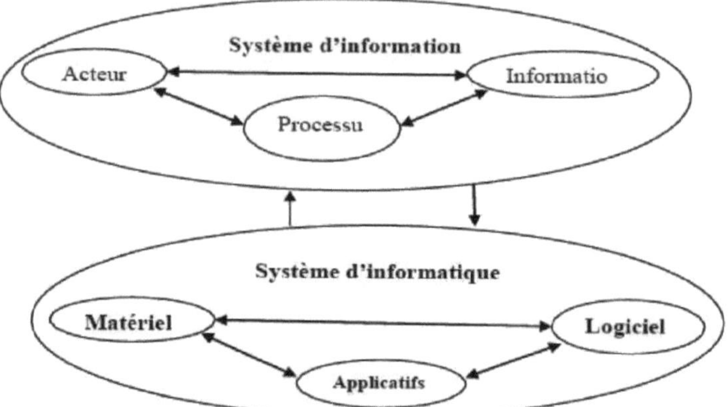

Figure 2: Information system and computer system (p. 17)

1.2 The Hospital Information System (HIS):

Having seen the basic concepts of an IS and its definitions, we will be able to approach the history and definitions of the hospital information system, its components, and then analyse it on several axes.

1.2.1 History of the HIS:

The current situation of the supply of Hospital Information Systems (HIS) has naturally been largely shaped by its past. It seems only natural to devote a chapter to a brief overview of the main stages in the development of HIS provision.

Given the characteristics of hospital IT, particularly the major weight of the public authorities and the State in the construction of the offer, this history has been marked and strongly marked by several ministerial circulars and by several reports emanating from various bodies: it is therefore through these circulars and reports that we will draw up a rapid overview of the last thirty years.

The main circulars that have shaped hospital IT are the following:

□ Circulars of 1950, computer science has undergone profound transformations. The transformation of computer hardware is major in terms of speed, power, reliability and miniaturisation. Today, IT has professional uses in all fields, as well as private uses. The development of the first HIS, mainly in the United States and in some

European countries such as the Netherlands, Sweden and Switzerland, dates back to the mid-1960s. This development follows the general evolution of information technology.

□ Circulars of 1970, the HIS according to a vertical approach, which is used in France, consists in copying the applications on the structures of the hospital. In the 1980s, HIS according to a horizontal and process-based approach, the horizontal approach consists of individualising the processes to be computerised. If the number of processes to be computerised remains low, the number of interfaces to be realised is controlled.

□ Circulars of 1990, the HIS according to a mixed approach consists, in a simplified way, of following a horizontal approach for the care units and a vertical approach for the technical platforms. This approach was often used in the nineties, in order to be able to computerise the radiology departments in hospitals first.

□ Circulars of 2000, the HIS according to an integrated approach where the HIS becomes more efficient and above all more collaborative. The approach is called integrated because the modules communicate with each other and are integrated into one and the same system. The interfaces are reduced because the HIS are, as far as possible, integrated into one and the same system. From the mid-2000's onwards, the concept of decision support was introduced.

□ Circulars from the year 2000, integration of decision support into HIS, decision support systems have been integrated into Information Systems since the beginning of the year 2000.

1.2.2 Definition of HIS:

Hospital information systems first appeared in France after the creation in 1991 of the PMSI information systems medicalisation programme.

The ministerial circulars n°275 of 6 January 1989 of the Ministry of Health defined the Information System of a health establishment can be defined "as the set of information, its circulation and processing rules necessary for its daily functioning, its management and evaluation methods as well as its strategic decision-making process".

HIS is one of the components of the Health Information System. According to Gerard Poncon, gives the following definition: "The hospital information system is an integral part of the hospital organisation "in perpetual evolution; it is capable, according to predefined rules and operating methods, of acquiring data, evaluating them, processing them using computer or organisational tools, and distributing information containing high added value to all the establishment's internal or external partners, collaborating in a common effort oriented towards a specific goal, namely the care of a patient and his recovery".

According to De goulet, "the Hospital Information System (HIS) can be defined as a computer system designed to facilitate the management of all medical and administrative information in a hospital".

The purpose of the HIS is to provide a tool for hospital managers who can finally have access to data on what their hospital actually produces; to become an instrument of quality assurance in hospitals because, by allowing relevant comparisons, it encourages the adoption of good practices.

1.2.3 The components of the HIS

The HIS is mainly composed of three systems which are :

□ The administrative system:

The administrative system allows for the admission of patients, the management of their movements within the hospital (beds, transfers between departments) known as "operational management", the administrative discharge of patients, invoicing (stay costs), etc. It has several sub-systems, among others:

• The accounting system: includes several sub-systems: supplier accounting, client accounting (in the case of the hospital, this is the accounting management of accommodation expenses), fixed asset management, etc., etc.

• The sub-system of daily hospital administration: deals with invoicing, personnel management, stock management and, in general, accounting.

□ The logistics system:

Includes all flows resulting from medical actions (prescriptions, results, transfers, archiving). It brings into play the establishment's various clinical services and technical platforms to support the activity of the healthcare team.

□ Medical-technical information systems:

The technical platform in the broadest sense includes all the examination platforms (laboratories, medical imaging, functional explorations, etc.), but also the central pharmacy, to a certain extent the resuscitation and intensive care departments.etc. It has several sub-systems which are :

- The medical action sub-system: Concerns the activity implemented by the health care team to respond to the patient's problem: the information gathered on the patient, the constitution and consultation of the patient's file, medical knowledge, decision-making.... processes, etc.

• Research and study sub-system: Works on groupings of records, provided they have been properly constituted, for epidemiological purposes or devaluation of the quality of care. feeding back into the medical knowledge or the administration and planning sub-systems.

• The hospital planning sub-system: With a more strategic vision, it is based on business analysis or hospital morbidity studies to make structural investment decisions. It is in relation with external entities (supervisory authorities, surrounding health care provision, health status of the population served, ...etc.).

These components are summarised in the following figure:

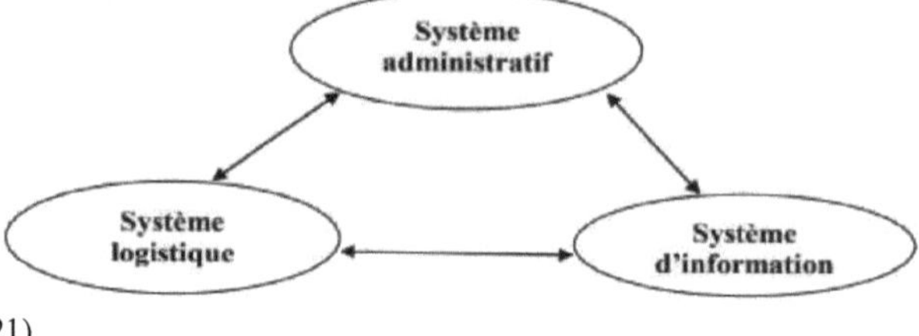

21)

Figure 3: Components of HIS

(Saidani & Taleb, p.

The hospital is in fact a fdddration of functionally distinct but not disjointed subsystems, within and between which information flows.

All these subsystems are interdependent and are largely focused on the patient's file. Thus, even if "medical" and "administrative" information are not collected by the same people, do not use the same procedures or knowledge, and do not focus on the same facts, medical action cannot be abstracted from administrative information, while the hospital cannot be properly managed without considering its purpose of care (quality of care, progress of knowledge, adaptation to the needs of the population).

1.2.4 Organisations concerned by the HIS

The term "HIS" refers explicitly to the internal information system of a health care organisation, especially hospitals. The institutions visited are typically :

- Hospitals or public structures ;
- Private clinics or structures.

Although having Information Systems, the term HIS will not be appropriate for other health organisations such as :

- Radiology centres;
- Medical biology analysis laboratories;
- The care centres ;
- Medical practices.

When the first Information Systems were installed in the establishments of
In the care sector, it is usual to differentiate between the Clinical Information System (CIS) containing the patient's clinical data, and the Hospital Information System (HIS) containing the patient's administrative entry data (entry, stay, movements, identity, address).

1.2.5 Approaches to analysing the hospital information system

The analysis of the hospital's information system can be carried out along several lines:

1.2.5.1. The components of the HIS environment :

As a result, a variety of players are involved directly or indirectly through the hospital information system, while external players include regulatory bodies, insurance companies, industrialists and the media; internal players are obviously patients and healthcare personnel (doctors, nurses, etc.). As for the internal players, these are the patients, the care staff (doctors, nurses, etc.), the administrative staff, etc. These players are shown in the following figure:

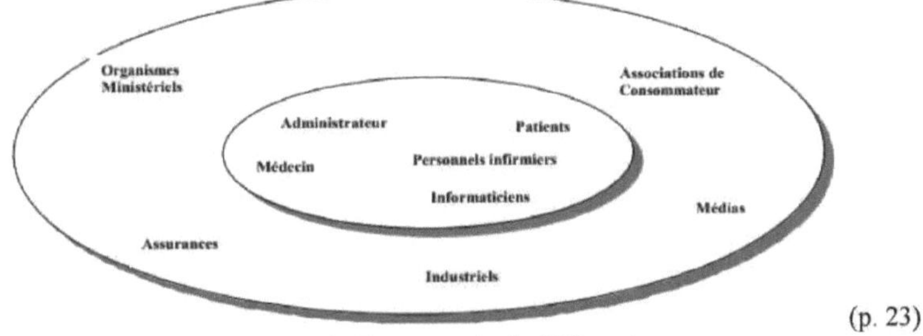

(p. 23)

Figure 4: The actors in the HIS environment

Comment: In analysing this figure, it must be concluded that the role of the computer specialist is not to be neglected in the process of patient care, especially as he is an actor on a par with the administrator, the patient, the doctor and the nurse in the rational management of the patient's administrative data by computerised means. As we have said, everyone has already understood that access to information in real time has a positive impact on patient care; hence the imperative presence of the computer system in an HIS.

2.2.5.2 Functional approach:

The HIS is subdivided into major functions, sub-functions such as: medical functions (computerised medical record, prescription of acts), logistical functions, financial functions, etc.

Advantage :

□ Simple to understand because we have a breakdown by trade, so immediate reading.

□ Corresponds often to the offer of the suppliers.

Inconvenient : □ Does not allow computerisation of processes that straddle several domains.

□ Illustration: prescription of medicines by the doctor, inseparable from its administration by the nurse, inseparable from the dispensing or validation by the pharmacist.

The figure below illustrates this analysis:

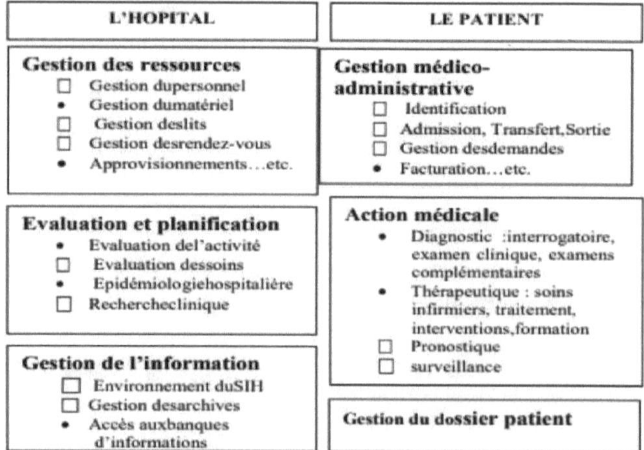

Figure 5: Functional analysis of HIS

(p. 23)

Comment: Although much more involved in **Information Management**, the IT specialist is involved in all the other functions of the HIS; hence the need for the IT department in a hospital centre which has IT specialists with a wide range of specialities as human resources.

2.2.5.3 Structural (topological) approach:

Division of the HIS according to the organisational division: care units, technical platform, administrative services.

Advantage :

□ Allows you to manage a target project □ Allows you to superimpose the workgroup to the department.

Example: setting up a speciality file in a cardiology department.

Inconvenient

- □ Risk of reaching a departmental HIS.
- □ Difficulty in advancing the logic of integration.
- □ Illustration: one medical file per care unit, with no communication with the administrative IT system and even less between them (continuity of care within a care sector).

In terms of information system analysis, each of these structures, whether medical or medico-technical, becomes a resource available to other structures or to the outside world, generating acts, producing information and consuming other resources. This analysis is summarised in the following figure:

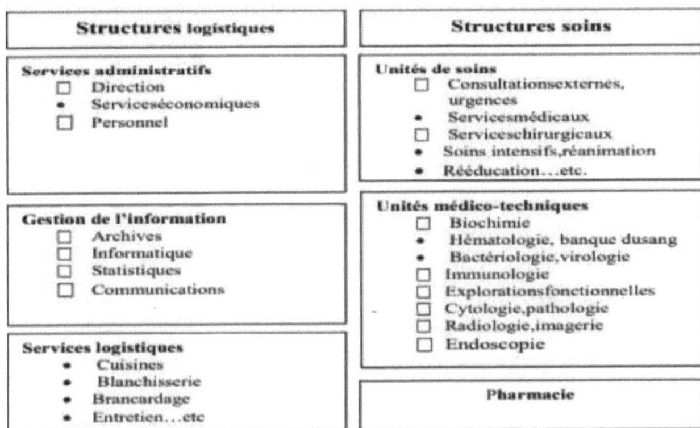

Figure 6: Structured analysis^ of HIS

(p. 25)

2.2.5.4 The main objectives of the HIS

HIS is important for the operation and management of a health care institution. It facilitates management, evaluation and planning. According to Kohler, the HIS has two main objectives: improving the quality of care and controlling costs.

In order to better understand the objectives of the latter, the following table is presented:

Table 1: Objectives of the HIS

Quality of the scans	• Improving communication • Reduction of waiting times • Dossier paiientintegre • Help in making donations
Neck control	• Reduction of the length of stay • Reduction of the lachiesadminisiraiives • Optimisation of resources

The hospital information system is an essential support for hospital management, it has a set of characteristics specific to health care institutions, it retains the fundamental elements that define any information system, but the success of an HIS is subject to several conditions. Among the most important are: a thorough knowledge of the flow of information in the hospital, a detailed analysis of the sociology of the organisation, a suitable hardware and software strategy and a fair estimate of the resources required.

1.2. The contribution of the HIS to improving hospital performance

This section is taken from Chapter III of the Authors' Memoir cited in the introduction to our first chapter.

The study conducted in 2018 by SAIDANI Nacera and TALEB Siham focused on in-depth empirical analysis to determine and explain, through a questionnaire, how the hospital information system contributes to improving performance at Bab El Oued University Hospital.

It should be pointed out, before continuing with this section, that the performance in question here can only be the result of a real HIS worthy of being called a 'Decision Support Tool', and therefore a *computerised* HIS.

2.1 The role of the hospital information system

2.1.1 The information system is a decision-making aid:

The Hospital Information System will enable managers to obtain the information they need to make decisions, to study the possible consequences of their decisions more easily, and to automate certain decisions.

2.1.2   The Hospital Information System is a tool for controlling revolution and health organisation:

The Hospital Information System will enable the detection of internal dysfunctions or abnormal situations so that this tool can be operational; the Information System must be the "collective шёшоие" of the organisation, keeping a constant trace of each piece of information.

2.1.3 The Hospital Information System is a coordination tool of différentes active hospital activities:

The Hospital Information System will also provide information on the present, which will be the same for all services and will be updated regularly. Everybody is informë in the same way according to their access to information: **Principle of 'Segregation of duties'** (Mbilizi, 2020) in the database technique.

For the researchers, the HIS finals numbered three (cLision, control and coordination), and are summarised in the following table:

Table 2: The three weaknesses of information systems

Purposes cTtin hospital information system

The decision

Control

Coordination

The information system allows a number of decisions to be automated, resulting in appropriate decisions.

11 also provides decision-makers with the necessary elements for decision-making and allows the consequences to be studied.

The image is visible from this one. [] has been made for the purpose of assisting the decision.

But the computer must never replace the decision-maker, especially since it is a vehicle for repetitive information and cannot provide all the information necessary for the most important decisions, which are exceptional in nature.

The information system should be the memory of the organization by processing the information about its past. This history of the situation allows a control of the organization's revolution by detecting abnormal situations in advance.

Ex daccounting
generalproduct
regular reporting of financial statements describing
all financial transactions carried out with third parties.
The information system must also trailer the information designing the present of Γ hop it al in
order to coordinate the action of different sub-systems Ex: systems
information interview! in order processing at
coordinating Taction of deliverers and patient accounting with representatives cellc.

(p. 109)

For dëcider, it is necessary to have information:

• Relevant

The organisation of which is adapted to the management needs of the health establishment;

• Reliable

They are trustworthy, true, accurate and up to date;

• Available

Existing and not concealed (structured information).

2.3 **The functions of the HIS as a tool for performance improvement**

The hospital is considered as a complex system, and every complex system is broken down into three sub-systems according to the generic decomposition proposed by LeMoigne.

The latter is called canonical model O.I.D. (Operator system / Information system / Decision system). These three sub-systems in the hospital environment are represented as follows:

The operating system provides data to the information system and receives execution messages. The data are always internal events for it, and the execution messages represent operations to be carried out. In a hospital, every structure that produces, manufactures, performs is an operating system.

The steering system, pergoit information, analyses it and generates new information of a particular type called decision.

The information system, on the other hand, provides the link between the different systems. Or it collects and stores information from the outside (e.g. a social security agreement or a ministerial circular) and information from the operating system (e.g. a prescription for a patient, a drug delivery note). This information is referred to as "events", external for the former and internal for the latter. It receives directives from the decision-making system, such as for example : The decision maker processes all the information that passes through him, putting the sender and recipient in contact and memorising it, and finally he provides information to the decision system, to inform it and give it the means to take it; to the operating system, so that it knows the decisions it has to execute; externally if the nature of the information so provides and if the decision-making system has ordered it to do so.

Therefore, the information system allows to collect, memorize, process and restore the different data of the organization in order to allow the steering system to perform its functions while ensuring its coupling with the operational system.

To this end, the information system must therefore transmit three types of information:

• Production information, which comes from the operating system and is most often of an elementary and repetitive type (patient identity, analysis results, hospital staff present, etc.).

• Guiding information, which allows us to take stock of the day-to-day objectives and is necessary for the administrative and medical management of the establishment.
• Steering information, from which long-term strategic options are established. The latter is either management information or medical statistical data, synthesised and defined over time, enabling hospital, administrative and medical decision-makers to perceive the main lines of development of the hospital beyond the less significant instantaneous variations.

All this information must be of general intrinsic quality, suitable for the use for which it was designed and selected. Here too, everyone may have his own opinion on these qualities, but it may not be useless to present the main ones:
- Hospital information should be symbolic;
- Hospital information must be of the highest intrinsic quality;
- Hospital information must be consistent;
- Hospital information must be accessible but confidential;
- Hospital information must be partially removable;
- Hospital information must be detailed but global;
- The information must be of a synthetic nature;
- The information must be presented in the information system in order to be coherent.

But all these briefly presented characteristics should not make us forget that information is a material which the decision-maker uses, among other analytical factors, to make his decision and that, finally, the availability of quality information does not mean that the decision taken will be relevant, timely and applicable.

In order to meet the needs of decision-makers, it is necessary to synthesize, reorganize and historize the production data of the information system in order to determine a sub-set of it related to hospital performance. The HIS therefore plays an essential role in the process of improving the quality of hospital services. Its importance lies in the fact that it reduces the uncertainty inherent to the latter, since the first characteristic of decisions is uncertainty. It also allows the analysis of the external and internal environment.

To analyse the external environment, the nature and quality of the links with other components of the health system are examined: Local hospitals, city medicine, ambulances, treatment rooms, screening, communication with the population, environmental hygiene and socio-cultural habits.

In order to analyse the internal environment (clinical and administrative performance), for a well-founded diagnosis, comparative studies are needed:
Comparison over time, in order to have a perception of the trends with analysis of the considerable deviations.

Comparison with other providers in order to be able to place oneself in relation to the average. It is clear that this evaluation requires indicators, in order to make strategic decisions.

It should be stressed that the information system is at the heart of hospital organisations' communication, as it structures, informs and codifies internal communication.

2.4 Qualities of a hospital information system

2.4.1 First quality: the rapidity of information transmission

This criterion is not to be considered in an absolute way. It means that the speed of information flow must be determined by the maximum time tolerable for decisions and the actions they entail to be carried out within compatible time limits.

This speed is made evolutive according to the considered moment, variable according to the nature of the activity and also according to the nature of the information itself. It is therefore a question of having the right speed of information transmission for each data and in a certain context.

2.4.2 Second quality: the reliability of the drive train.

Reliability is a quality that must be absolute. It means that the information must be relevant and complete.

☐ The relevance of the information

This means that information should only be presented in the system to the extent that it is relevant to him.

☐ The information must be complete

This means that partial information cannot be processed or may lead to processing errors.

2.5 The types of performance and the factors influencing them in the Bab ElOued C.H.U.

Any organisation that is vigilant in its evolution must identify the different types of performance and it must constantly measure the latter because it is a matter of topicality for all managers.

The performance of the Bab El Oued university hospital centre, it is a question of studying the performance of an organisation and not of an individual, an actor or a process.

Performance is studied in the light of the hospital's objectives and the expectations of the players, taking into account the context in which it is achieved, hence the need to identify these three aspects (objectives, expectations and context) before analysing the performance.

As regards expectations, it is a question of studying how the institution's performance can enable the expectations expressed by the actors to be met and the way in which expectations can be translated into performance criteria.

☐ **Performance characteristics**

- It can be measured, hence the need to construct or use appropriate qualitative or quantitative indicators;

- It is assessed, based on comparisons over time (changes in the value of the organisation's indicators over several years) and/or in space (using the values of indicators from comparable organisations when available);

- It can be explained by internal factors (linked to the actors) or external factors (linked to environmental fluctuations).

Among the types of performance existing in the Bab El Oued University Hospital: organisational performance, technical performance, managerial performance, social performance and economic performance.

3.4 The need for hospital information systems to improve performance

Hospital information systems play an important role in improving the efficiency and effectiveness of hospital performance. In fact, in the decision-making process, they allow to eliminate the inefficiency of various medical and administrative decisions, according to the World Health Organization (WHO) the inefficiency of decisions taken in health care institutions is the result of the lack of information, as well as of the tools responsible for their collection, transport and use, indexing and processing to make them appropriate, given that information systems are used in different cases involving medical decision, in this case, medical prescription, medicine for a patient suffering from a disease or control of the epidemic through the development of a major health strategy. In addition, hospital information systems remain paramount in the medical process, hence the importance of clarifying the areas in which health performance and decision-making are improved:

□ Hospital information systems provide the basis for an accurate health map for the country as a whole in terms of prevalence and its causes with precision and speed. For example, the decision-maker needs to have hundreds of scattered messages and contradictory data at his disposal to remain within the limits of the spread of a specific disease such as the hepatitis virus.

□ Thanks to the hospital information system, the decision-maker can immediately identify the state of the inventory, in particular, medicines and medical supplies in all hospitals and health centres, and concludes including information on the needs of each hospital or health centre. In addition, there is a unified list of purchases at the national level proposed by the wholesale markets.

□ The information system makes it possible to identify the level of performance of all health care institutions in the country to avoid common medical inconveniences and errors, as the health care institution must use a medical record for each patient, as it is considered the first person to judge the performance of any part of the institution. The health record makes it possible to collect and record the performance of the practices of the medical community in an objective, complete and accurate manner.

□ Through this system, health planners will be able to monitor the financial performance of hospitals in real terms and expenditures. Any overestimation of costs on the basis of standard systems of treatment costing and drug treatment costs incurred. As it has therapeutic facilities in many countries of the developed world.

□ This will also facilitate the extraction of precise statistics on the results, number and percentage of geographical operations, patient mortality and quality in different disciplines, then the analysis of these statistics for each period in order to detect weaknesses and thus avoid them. then monitor the input of information on treatment and the strengthening of the health decision making process. to allow better patient satisfaction.

3.5 The place of the HIS in hospital performance

Information technology has become an indispensable tool for organisations seeking competition and excellence in their production. their results. as well as the efficiency and effectiveness of their performance. organisations have hastened to create the groundwork to implement them. Indeed, the use of this tool is creating unprecedented opportunities in several areas. such as upgrading performance. improving administrative decisions. simplifying and facilitating processes and optimising the use of manpower for its significant contribution to financial systems. through the implementation of numerous actions and changes (Structure. operations. management of the organization) and train users in its use to ensure its operation to achieve effective performance standards which is the main objective of any organization. it should be noted that the relationship between the use of computerized information systems and professional performance is as follows:

1. To improve functionality strongly and efficiently by getting routine and consequential work done quickly, accurately and at low cost.

2. Reduce the child's routine workload by enabling him or her to exploit this time in the strategic planning and policy development of the organization, which has contributed to the efficiency and effectiveness of senior management.

3. To improve the morale of employees by motivating them to become more loyal and strengthen their sense of belonging to the organisation. this is achieved through easy access to information, which contributes to promotion. as well as their participation in the decision-making process.

4. Information technology enables organizations to gain a competitive advantage in the marketplace. By paying increased attention to research and development to contribute to the improvement and development of individual resources.

5. Dissemination and reinforcement of organisational culture and administrative guidelines at the highest levels of any organisation. Indeed. the results of their management processes have an important role in the evolution towards the use of information technology. Thus, this appears in the form of the organisational work environment and the collective adoption of the administrative process.

6. Effective decision-making and quality improvement are the result of an efficient administrative communication process within and outside the organisation. and the improvement of the process of coordination and alliance between the different levels and administrative units to achieve the objectives of the organisation.

In addition, the application of modern information systems has a positive effect on the efficiency of employees and an impact on the speed of completion of work. through administrative flexibility. and the great importance attached to evaluating the performance of the organisation's staff.

1.3. Partial conclusion

In this chapter, we have discussed the theory relevant to information systems in general, and hospital information systems in particular.

Using the work done by Saidani Nacera and Taleb Siham, we can conclude:

The IS is increasingly ëvolutif following the complex^ and dëveloppement organizations.

Information is the raw material of any organisation. For gërer it is imperative to have a real IS that can provide the information needed in real time. The IS in a hospital structure is commonly called HIS.

The HIS is a tool to help hospital managers, who can finally have access to data on the production of their establishment, to become an instrument of quality assurance in hospitals because, by allowing relevant comparisons, it encourages the adoption of good practices.

The HIS is a decision-making aid, a tool for controlling revolution and coordinating the active population. In the hospital environment, as in any structure, an information system must be fast and reliable in the transmission and processing of information.

Thus, it becomes impëratif to be reassured that the health structure has a quality HIS for, not only the best quality of hospital management, but also the best quality of patient care.

Chapter Two: Description of the study setting: Brief presentation of *New Hope Hospital* (Musiwa, Mutayongwa, Alliance, Burakali, & Abale, 2020)

New Hope Hospital is a network of private hospitals located in the province of South Kivu in the Democratic Republic of Congo, Central Africa.

This network has been established since 2015 and has two modern hospitals whose main mission is to provide quality care to the population of the Great Lakes region as well as expatriate staff. One is located in the centre of Kavumu in the Kabare Territory and the other in the city of Bukavu, Commune of lbanda.

2.1. General

Created on 06 June 2015 in Kavumu, Kabare Territory, South Kivu Province by Dr Pascal NAMEGABE LURHAKUMBIRA, New Hope for Congo is a simplified cooperative society under Congolese law, with only one hospital installed in the centre of Kavumu but in view of its praise and satisfactory achievements, the beneficiaries of the services of New Hope Hospital have requested that there be an extension in Bukavu, so New Hope Hospital Bukavu will see the light of day on March 13, 2017.

Its objectives are as follows:

- The fight against sexual and gender-based violence by educating the population to change mentalities;
- Psychosocial care and legal support in cases of rape and gender-based violence;
    - The promotion of mother and child health;
    - The prevention of conflicts and genocides;
    - Economic empowerment of women.

It is a cooperative company that owns hospitals called New Hope Hospital.

The first hospital was opened in Kavumu in 2015 in the Kabare territory and organises several medical services for the well-being of the population. Since then, New Hope for Congo has launched a project to fight against sexual and gender-based violence by organising campaigns to change mentalities in the groups of Mudaka, Rwabika (Miti), Bugorhe (Kavumu), Irhambi (Katana) in collaboration with an organisation that has been working on the issue of sexual and gender-based violence. ашёпсаше дёпошшёе Jewish World Watch. The target groups of these projects are: the Congolese l'Армёе, the Congolese National Police, former child soldiers and members of groups армёs who have become bikers, the ёcoles and universities, magistrates and lawyers, women's groups, civil sociëtë and the entire population in gënëral.

Psychosocial follow-up and legal support for all cases of sexual and gender-based violence are part of the project's activities.

The New Hope for Congo hospitals offer various services within its dëpartements including :
- Pediatrics,
- Gynecology and obstetrics,
- Surgery and oral surgery,
- Internal medicine,
- Medical imaging,
- Dermatology,
- ENT
- Ophthalmology,
- The pharmacy,
- The laboratory,
- I . administration and
- Scientific research.

2.2 Organisation chart of the New Hope Hospital Medical Centre *(202i)*

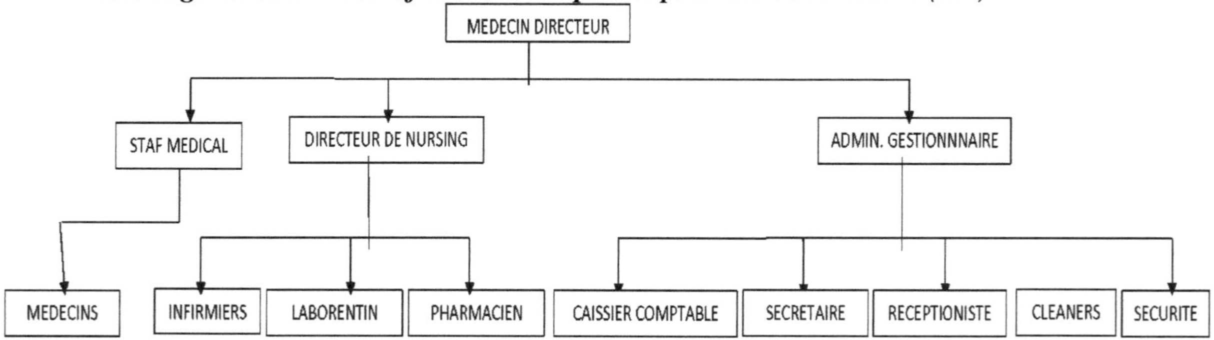

Figure 7: NHH organisation chart

2.3. Organisation and operation of NHH

The hospital centre is managed by the Senior Manager, who is a promoter and statutory founder. It is therefore an approved private hospital centre.

It comprises two medical structures, one in Bukavu and one in Kavumu; each structure is run by a Medical Director. NHH explicitly has two Medical Directors, one in Bukavu and one in Kavumu. Both report to the Director Manager or his delegate, locally called the Director "Director".

The administrative and financial management for both medical training courses is in the hands of a single agent called the Managing Administrator.

The data management of both hospitals is the function of the Executive Secretary, who produces all the necessary reports, statistics, invoices, and consumption reports, as well as purchase orders and requisitions on a daily basis. He is commonly referred to as the "Lung, centraliser, data bank manager" or the "computer specialist".

The security agents in collaboration with the reception are in charge of the reception and orientation of patients.

The nursing staff consists of doctors, nurses, laboratory technicians and pharmacists.

Chapter three:
Study of the existing information system at New Hope Hospital

3.1. History of the IT department and the strategic plan

(Zirimwabagabo, Kisulamilwa, & Bahogwerhe, 2020)

When it was founded, the promoter of NEW HOPE HOSPITAL did not have in mind the IT service among so many services of its medical training. It only had the main mission of providing quality health care to the local population.

The pre-2019 organizational chart of New Hope Hospital only included the following services/agents:

1) The Medical Director ;
2) The administrator manager ;
3) Doctors ;
4) Accounting ;
5) Nurses, laboratory assistants and pharmacists ;
6) Reception ;
7) Security ;
8) The cleaning service.

Little by little, medical electronic equipment required regular maintenance; hence the need for the Manager to add to the previous services the service of maintenance of medical kits under the responsibility of two electronic and electrical technicians in order to regulate the electrical installation and other energy solutions, preventive and curative maintenance of medical equipment.

One year later, New Hope Hopital sees itself with several subscribers to its services, who ask for invoices, consumption records, medical files (diagnosis, history of the disease, medical history, anamnesis complements, medical reports, evolution, treatment, lab results, medical imaging, etc.) daily, weekly, monthly, etc. when this is required for hundreds of patients.

The management of human resources (files, contracts, training, promotions, pay...) has created a variety of information to manage. Relations with the state services have also imposed an adequate management of the appropriate information (follow-up of tax payments, CNSS contributions, etc.).

The Ministry of Health will require New Hope Hospital to deliver weekly, monthly, quarterly, and yearly various administrative reports (attendance rates, primary care statistics, surgery statistics, maternity, chronic diseases and other pathologies).

The Manager also, not being a regular employee in his companies, felt the need to know with precision, albeit from a distance, the exact number of patients per category who attended his hospitals daily, monthly and annually, how many were Ho8p11a118ë8, opёгёз, how many were accoиcЬё? Which ones? How much money do they get into the hospital? Who consumes more? Who are the profitable agents and budgëtivores?

These kinds of new problems have ёdictë the setting up of a new service: the IT service, which unfortunately due to the limit of means, has ётё subsisted by the recruitment of an *Executive Secretary,* who must obligatorily have a qualification and

skills in compëtences ëlevëes computer science for information management,
according to the management policy of New Hope Hospital.

With the active participation of all staff members, the management secretary plays
the role not only of the hospital's administration, but also of the IT department. This
situation of administrative organisation makes it difficult to implement the stratëgique
plan of the IT department of NEW HOPE HOSPITAL.

3.2. Master plan and organisation chart

The master plan is a rather large (between 10 and 150 pages) technical document, ёстй by the
IT managers who do not say where they are located in relation to the management gënërale,
but dëcrivent only what everyone does in relation to the IT department (Bulabula, p. 28).

Under the supervision of the Executive Secretary, who is responsible for the IT
department (although a virtual service), meetings are held at the end of each quarter, in which
each member of staff explains the difficulties presented by his or her IT tool or expresses new
software or matëriels needs. With the opinions of all departments (all ëtant members of the IT
department according to the organisational policy), the management secretary, an IT expert,
assesses the needs and sets up a corrective action plan:

The master plan is generally the prerogative of the management secretary, the computer
scientist compëtent, head of the IT department. The Secretariat of New Hope Hospital makes
an effort to submit projects for computerization and system improvement although the
company is essentially not concerned with computerization. These include :

^ The comptabilitë : automatisës input-output management moddles ;

^ Applications for service reports ;

^ Personnel applications: payroll ;

^ Pharmacy and laboratory stock management ;

^ Clinical applications;

^ 'OFFICE' applications: patient file management, archiving, confidentialitë ;

^ Sëcuritë of the donirees ;

^ Administration and network security ;

^ The choice and purchase of computer equipment according to the latest
technological developments;

^ The validation of new computer ëquipements.

3.3. Material, human and financial resources

1. HUMAN RESOURCES

The IT department of New Hope Hospital includes the following staff:

^ The executive secretary: computer scientist, head of department ;

^ The management: the director and the director manager who give professional
orientations;

^ Administration: 1 'Administrator Manager who gives business orientations on the
day-to-day management aspect of the organisation. The current GA is qualified
and competent in computer science;

^ Doctors and nurses: they provide guidance in the management of medical and
treatment records of patients, which may be computerised;

^ Laboratory and pharmacy technicians: they clarify on the management of stock of
laboratory inputs and drugs;

^ Accounting and cash management: these agents participate in the elaboration of
models for cash management and bookkeeping;

^ Reception: they take part in the elaboration of orientation documents for patients in the different departments of the hospital;

^ Security is participating in the implementation of the tdld tools for monitoring movements within the hospital.

2. HARDWARE, SOFTWARE AND NETWORK RESOURCES

New Hope Hospital is equipped with computers, medical equipment and offices (printers, photocopiers, scanners). The properties of the hospital's computers are within the norms.

On the network aspect, wireless technology (LAN, WLAN, routers, switches and cables). In NEW HOPE HOSPITAL there is easy and permanent access to the internet.

The operating system: Windows and linux; desktop applications: MS-Word, Excel, Publisher, Power Point; DBMS: MS-ACCESS, browsers, and e-mail address for e-mail, Excel workbooks for patient follow-up. All these tools are designed, proposed and implemented internally by the Executive Secretary.

3. FINANCIAL RESOURCES

NEW HOPE HOSPITAL's IT department does not have its own budget. All its needs are submitted to the Accounting and Management Administrator, who appreciate them and ensure their financing.

The agents have their monthly salaries. The hospital, in order to bear all its expenses, depends only on the medical care paid by the patients or their health insurers.

3.4. Situation and gap analysis

The IT department assigns several missions. You already know this and we have demonstrated it in the strategic plan. We have shown, through the IT master plan, what the service does on a daily basis.

It should be remembered that the clear objective of this study is to assess the risks and weaknesses in the *management of* patient *administrative data in* particular, and HIS information in general, as described theoretically in Chapter 1.

Indeed, as far as the IT department is concerned, although considered as such by the manager, in reality it is an erroneous term within New Hope Hospital. In the true sense, the IT department of New Hope Hospital substitutes itself as a secretariat because, as already said, an IT department is made up of HR, all qualified and competent, with various specialities, who execute the IT master plan with the material, software and financial resources at their disposal.

Regarding the application system, NHH's information system suffers from the inexistence of a website and web applications for the hospital; and yet the web is a very important technology for the digital opening of any organisation in the context of making itself known to the world, but also the online management of remote structures (Bukavu and Kavumu for the case of New Hope Hospital). Moreover, the batches of information brought in on paper by different services in order to be captured and stored in files on computers does not mean computerisation. Computerisation implies the existence of a database and applications shared between different services that allow each actor to perform the tasks specific to him in order to update the system in real time. Concretely, it seems that NHH's HIS is computerised if :

-   When the doctor registers a patient in his consulting room, the database manager will note this at the same time;

-   When a sample is taken at the laboratory in Kavumu, Bukavu, one immediately
    becomes aware of it;
-   In order to present the various reports, the agent concerned simply clicks on an
    interface of the application, which, with the help of SQL queries developed by the
    designers, prints out the necessary output reports;
-   Invoices and statements of patients' consumption were managed automatically by
    the computer system;
    -   The hospitalized patients were tele-monitored by means of expert systems;
-   There were graphical interfaces for each service to enter the necessary data
    allowing the automatic generation of the patient record, the surveillance record,
    the ultrasound protocol, the operating protocol, the parthogram, the lab voucher,
    ...;
    -   There were clinical applications for decision support, etc.
And yet none of the above is operational in New Hope Hospital's HIS.

As for data, we cannot talk about it if we ever do without databases. Computer
databases are used in a large number of companies to store, organise and analyse data
(www.lebigdata.fr). Databases are stored as files or a set of files on a magnetic disk,
cassette, optical disk, or other type of storage device.
One of the things we have to remember is that the standards of database technology
learned at the Faculty are of prime importance:
-   The database is managedd by a database management system whichh is a software
    program for creating the database andd its objects,,for writing andd structuring the
    data,,for manipulating,,storing,,processing,,disseminating andd securing the data;
-   A database must have addquates graphical user interfaces to bridge the gap
    between it and its users;
    -   Sharing of information between users ;
    -   Communication anddrelationships betweenn data (relational models) ;
    -   La gestion des privileges (Segregation of duties) ;
    -   Requests for exploitation are used as decision-making tools;
    -   Reports, etc.

3.5.   *Inventory of databases at New Hope Hospital*

Databases or databases?
New Hope Hospital usually has data banks. Generally, these are files of an
organisational nature (spreadsheets, documents, presentations, etc.).
Which DBMS are used?
As a database management system is recognized, New Hope Hospital did not use one
five years ago, yet the need for information continues to be expressed. In order to
meet these needs in whole or in part, the IT department, in view of the multiple
responsibilities assigned to it by means of a single qualified agent (the executive
secretary), generally uses the MS-Excel spreadsheet, which, until proven otherwise, is
not a database management system.
Are there graphical interfaces for interaction between the database and users?
One of the fundamental qualities of a database is the rigour in its control of the data
entered by users (types of data, their formats, sizes and self-completion). Obviously,
this is only possible in programming thanks to the rigorously impldmenting forms;
however, despite the possibility to implement even forms for saving data on an MS-

Excel sheet, New Hope Hospital does not have user-friendly interfaces.

***What is the user privilege management policy in* place?**

We are well aware that the principle of "Segregation of duties" on which the management of user privileges is based aims to limit the access rights of users, and especially as we are dealing here with a health professional, the patient's data must remain confidential. Both of us may have the right to access the hospital's patient attendance database, but we do not necessarily have the same use for the same purpose. You can use it to view statistics without having the right to add or modify data.

Unfortunately, the Excel workbooks used by New Hope Hospital are only secured by a password at the door of any authorized user. Consequence: the administrator manager, by the fact that he only has the password of the opening of the spreadsheet or the Exeel sheet, can delete taehes which are only specific to the Medeein director, the executive secretary or the accountant. At this level, we note that the principle of "Segregation of duties" is not guaranteed.

Is it possible to describe and structure the data?

It is at this level that the eoneeptor defines the data type of an attribute, its format, its default value and its size.

The Data/Validation tab of the Exeel software used by New Hope Hospital, offers this possibility: one can define the type of data, the size, the min and max value as well as the messages in eas of input errors; unfortunately the help and the user guide are still pending; hence this tool is not at all reliable for the description and the structuring of the data as an essential quality of a database.

Is it possible to apply the relationship between data: relationships between tables or sheets?

Absolutely, if one is competent, there are Excel lists that derive from this or that sheet. But unfortunately, users at New Hope Hospital do not have an eompetenee. Each time a new Excel sheet is started, the expert has to be involved: the management secretary. But the users are not used to it themselves, as they may not have received any internal or external professional training in this field.

What about dissemination and data sharing?

New Hope Hospital uses WhatsApp, GMAIL, Drive, ... to exchange data between users. At this level, there is no multi-user, multi-station aspeet, changing and permanently updating data. Also, it should be noted that physical resources or networks playing the role of tempo to transfer data between devices may be missing. A user is able to send the files from his PC to his phone in order to send it to the management via WhatsApp, GMAIL, Drive etc. Can't we miss a USB stick or Bluetooth? How can I access the changes in real time? This is also a problem to report at New Hope Hospital in its database management!

In short, we found weaknesses in database management at New Hope Hospital. These shortcomings include the following:

3.6. *Diagnostic weaknesses/risks* :

- NHH's information system is manual ;
- In reality, there is no IT service within NHH;
- There are no real databases in New Hope Hospital, there are only databases (and only organizational files);There are no database management systems, but their

role is no longer to be demonstrated;
- No interface to facilitate data entry and input control by users, hence data typing problems, which biases the arithmetic and logical calculations on data, i.e. data processing problems;
    - Lack of security of their data banks;
    - Lack of description and structuring of the objects in their databases;
- Lack of relational databases, yet this is where we are now with database technology: the organisation is technologically behind;
    - Absence of web applications facilitating multi-user access to data.

3.7. *Partial conclusion*

An information system is made up of resources: material, immaterial and personnel who participate in the collection, processing, storage and dissemination of information.

Since the IS is the raw material of a company system, it is therefore imperious to have an adequate IS to guarantee the performance of its management.

With the current evolution of technology, artificial intelligence with expert systems that incarnates the knowledge of a human expert in a given field, helps to make rational decisions in its management (Murhula, 2019); hence the need for a computer system in an organizational information system that contributes to the performance of management.

The absence of automatic information processing software at New Hope Hospital leads to confirm the hypothesis that its *hospital information system is manual.*

Chapter four: Proposed solutions
4.0. Introduction

We did not survey all the health structures in the Democratic Republic of Congo to judge the quality of their HIS. However, despite the efforts made by some Congolese hospitals, particularly the provincial general hospitals of reference, some studies state that the majority of hospitals in the DRC have manual HIS: The article from the ULB cites in the state of the question of this work as the crowning testimony.

New Hope Hospital, which is the field of our study, is not sheltered from the ddfi dvoqud; this is why, as a university setting, we want to propose a certain number of solutions which we consider to be progressive and sustainable, with a view to obtaining an HIS for better medical care, given the high rank of this medical centre among the private hospitals in the province of South Kivu.

4.1. Existing solutions

Here, we will list a number of computer tools to assist in decision-making, i.e. more specifically medical or clinical software which already exists and is used elsewhere in health structures.

Open source software (OSS) is the fundamental criterion for the choice of software to enable the organisation's IT department to adapt it to their own business process or HIS, as it has free access to the source code of this software.

Free software respects the following freedoms (Diane, 2016) :

- Free to use the software as you wish (freedom 0) ;
- You are free to access the code, to study how it works, to modify it so that it performs your computer tasks as you wish (freedom 1);
- Free to redistribute copies of the software (Freedom 2);
- You are free to redistribute copies of your modified versions to others.

Indeed, the following table describes some of the software about which we have had access to the knowledge stock open to the scientific and professional public:

Table 3: Some medical or clinical software

Software	Platform	Developer	Features	Constraints	Comment	Source of information
CERHIS	Android	AEDES	- Computerisation of medical and administrative registers and documents ; - Follow-up of the patient's progress ; - Data transmission between different services	- Electricity supply ; - Local Wifi network for data transfer	-Installs a HGR Roi Baudouin, CS Bolingo and Kitoko (ZS Masina I in Kinshasa) since December 2017	www.Cerhis.org

Software	Platform	Developer	Features	Constraints	Comment	Source of information
			and user workstations		-Was in progress installation at the HPGR Goma in 2019	
Software	Platform	Developer	Features	Constraints	Comment	Source of information
OpenClinic GA	Windows, Linux, Xen	Medical eXchange Solutions	- Statistics and analysis ; - HRM ; - Planning system ; - Management of radiological and pathological results; - Laboratory order entry and results management with LOINC support; - Document management ; - Inventory management ; - Clinical Thesaurus 3 BT with management of ICD10 and ICPC-2 ; - SNomed CT coding support ; - Complete management of the ADT HL7 ; - The billing system ; - Management of public and private health insurance in Central Africa; - Identification of fingerprints with the help of the Digital Persona Library	Installation requirements are unclear	- It is a free software package ; - It may be sufficient to have the HIS computerized within NHH alone.	www.limswiki.o rg/index.php/ Op enClinic GA
Software	Platform	Developer	Features	Constraints	Comment	Source of information

OS patient	Multiplateforme		- Clinical documentation ; - Records management ; - Patient administration ; - Entering orders ; - Invoicing ; - Planning, etc.		- Web-based ; - Languages : English and German	https://source for ge.net/project s/p atientos

Comment : Any hospital concerned about improving its IS is called upon to appropriate one of the medical software available in the health sector, especially free software. For New Hope Hospital, we recommend the implementation of one of the software described in the previous table.

4.2. Proposal of project solutions

It is true that data banks, being organisational files, their importance is not to be questioned. But they must be used in a way that guarantees the security, description, structure and typing of the data. The Excel spreadsheet plays a capital role for New Hope Hospital if its users have all the competences to answer the raised concerns. Thus, as a first step, we recommend *the retraining of the IT staff.*

As far as the IT department is concerned, a Bachelor's Degree in Management Information Technology, the executive secretary, cannot alone meet all the IT needs expressed by the various departments of the hospital. If he is strong in analysis, design and programming (let's say), is he also strong in networks and security? In maintenance? In design? In telecommunications? Artificial intelligence? Thus, we recommend to New Hope Hospital the creation of another new department: *the IT department and to equip it with at least three other qualified and competent, but also multidisciplinary agents.* This service will have to set up an IT master plan for the organisation and will have to have a budget for its operation. It cannot necessarily function well by paying the salaries of the staff; a heading for the needs of this service in the hospital's budget forecast is needed for its smooth functioning.

As far as the setting up of databases is concerned, *theMS-ACCESS software* is indicated for use in the management of office databases. There are some IT needs that require the design and implementation of a database in MS-ACCESS to meet the standards referred to earlier in this work.

A website for the hospital's advertising is not enough for its daily management, so it is necessary. There are reports that are sent to WhatsApp, GMAIL, ... which should be generated automatically by web applications, hence we recommend *web applications to* New Hope Hospital.

4.3. Partial conclusion

The analysis carried out has thoroughly proved that manual IS cannot contribute to the performance of a hospital centre, yet it has been scientifically proven that the best HIS have an impact on the performance of public and private hospitals.

The weaknesses diagnosed in the NHH HIS can be solved by the proposals previously formulated; hence we confirm our second hypothesis that *a computerised information system is the most suitable for rational data management and increased patient monitoring.*

General Conclusion

As a computer scientist currently working in the health sector because our discipline is omnipotent, we pay particular attention to the hospital information system because, as we have already demonstrated, the IS is considered to be the backbone of any company system.

With this in mind, we set out to explore scientific research on the *analysis of the hospital information system in the DRC: the case of New Hope Hospital,* during which we analysed the quality of the HIS of the medical centre under study in order to make an objective and scientific judgement, according to which we found that the majority of HIS in the DRC are *manual,* and that of New Hope Hospital bears witness to this.

In order to contribute to the improvement of the quality of patient care in our entirety, we have proposed a *computerised* HIS, thanks to the IT resources that already exist and the solution projects that we have reformulated.

In view of New Hope Hospital's high standing in the health sector in the city of Bukavu, we asked ourselves the following questions about its HIS:

❖ *What information system exists within New Hope Hospital?*

❖ *What can be the optimal information system to provide the latter with for the rational management of its data and the increased monitoring of patients?*
  The following hypotheses have been made:

❖ Despite the presence of computers, printers, scanners, office software and other electronic equipment available at New Hope Hospital, given the absence of appropriate applications and databases for automatic data processing, *the existing information system at New Hope Hospital would be manual.*

❖ Given the granularity of the information to be managed in this hospital, the total treatment of humans exposes them to risks that are no longer to be demonstrated, *a computerised information system would be the most appropriate for rational data management and increased patient monitoring.*

The result achieved by the combination of *analytical and structural-functional* methods, and the techniques of interview, observation, documentation, etc., we have confirmed our hypotheses.

Difficulties encountered

Apart from minor financial difficulties (cost of research, data entry and printing, etc.) and some interference from the heads of our surveys, the major difficulty we encountered during the conduct of this project was the impossibility of extending our field of study, which was limited by the means and resources needed to survey a large number of hospitals in the DRC in order to draw a sample in line with the population as a whole.

In order to get around these constraints, we have carried out research at New Hope Hospital and searched the existing literature in order to investigate the state of the hospitals in the DRC as identified by the research of our predecessors.
As for the financial constraints, we have allocated the necessary funds, and with the support of some people of good will, we have completed the work.

Finally, one of the admitted limitations of this work is the limitation of the sample size, which is why we are proposing further research on HIS in the DRC, involving a large number of hospitals in the sample by province.

Bibliographic

1. Bakoben, S. (2009). *Patient management in a clinic in Java.*
2. Bulabula, K. D. (2016). *IT Audit Course. Bukavu Institute of Pedagogical Supervision.* Bukavu.
3. Diane, B. A. (2016, April). Open source HIS software: a solution for starting this type of project (HIS) in hospitals in the South in particular. *research gate,* 6-16. Rdcupdrd on https://www.researchgate.net/publication/308305897
4. *difference-entre-donnee-et-information.* (2018, Aout 4). Rdcupdrd sur WayToLearnX: https://www.waytol earnx .com
5. M. Abdoul, A. B. (2020). *Implementation of a web application for the management of patients in the Internal Medicine Department of the EL HADJI AHMADOUSAKHIRINDIEGUENE DE THIES Regional Hospital Centre.*
6. Mbilizi, D. M. (2020). *Information Systems Audit Course. Second Degree in Business Informatics. ULGL 2019-2020.* Bukavu.
7. Ministere des Solidarites et de la Sante. (2011, November). *Hopital-Numeric.* Rdcupdre sur Solidarites Sante Gouvernement Francais: https://www.solidarites-sante.gouv.fr
8. Murhula, G. K. (2019). *Courses in Artificial Intelligence and expert systems. L1 IG. ULGL. 2018-2019.* Bukavu, South Kivu, Democratic Republic of Congo.
9. Musiwa, P. M., Mutayongwa, M. K., Alliance, C. B., Burakali, J. B., & Abale, J. A. (2020). *Report of an IT audit carried out at New Hope Hospital from 28 October to 02 November 2020.* Practical work of the Information Systems Audit course, Free University of the Great Lakes, Higher and University Education, Bukavu. Accessed on February 04, 2021
10. Nalliat, R. (n.d.). *analysis-system-enterprise.* Retrieved from Cadre Dirigeant Magazine: https://www.cadre-dirigeant-magazine.com
11. New Hope Hospital. (2015). *Organizational chart.*
12. New Hope Hospital. (2021). *Organizational chart.*
13. Oumar, C. B. (2010). *Implementation of a hospital information system in French-speaking Africa: Cinz@n, study and validation of the model in Mali.* Accessed on February 2, 2021.
14. Reix, R. (1995, February 2). *cours-systemes-d-information-et-methode-merise.* Retrieved from Free Courses: https://www.cours-gratuit.com
15. Sabrina, G. (2015). *Development of the hospital information system through one of the eight principles of quality management.* Morocco.
16. Saidani, N., & Taleb, S. (2018). *Hospital information systems and hospital performance: a closely-linked study. Cas du CHUde mohamedLamine Debaghine.*
17. иbB-Coopёрайоп. (2019). Cerhis, IT tool adaptё for the management of hospitals in the DRC. *Vision, Missions and Values,* 1.
18. Wikipedia. (n.d.). DoniK'e (computer science). 1.
19. Zirimwabagabo, T. C., Kisulamilwa, G. N., & Bahogwerhe, D. M. (2020, November 2). On the existence of the IT department within NHH. (J. B. Burakali, Interviewer)

Table of contents

More
Books!

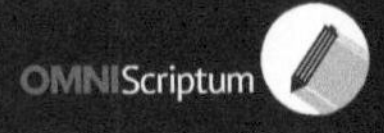

OMNIScriptum

Printed by Books on Demand GmbH, Norderstedt / Germany

Printed by Books on Demand GmbH, Norderstedt / Germany